& iPhone® Apps

FOR

DUMMIES®

MINI EDITION

by Bob LeVitus, Joe Hutsko, Barbara Boyd, and Nancy Muir

WILEY

John Wiley & Sons, Inc.

Incredible iPad® & iPhone® Apps For Dummies®, Mini Edition

Published by
John Wiley & Sons, Inc.
111 River Street
Hoboken, NJ 07030-5774
www.wiley.com

Copyright © 2012 by John Wiley & Sons, Inc., Hoboken, New Jersey

Published by John Wiley & Sons, Inc., Hoboken, New Jersey

Published simultaneously in Canada

For general information on our other products and services, please contact our Customer Care Department within the U.S. at 877-762-2974, outside the U.S. at 317-572-3993, or fax 317-572-4002.

For technical support, please visit www.wiley.com/techsupport.

Wiley also publishes its books in a variety of electronic formats. Some content that appears in print may not be available in electronic books.

ISBN 978-1-118-47969-8

Manufactured in the United States of America

10 9 8 7 6 5 4 3 2

WILEY

Contents

• •

Publisher's Acknowledgments

We're proud of this book; please send us your comments at
http://dummies.custhelp.com. For other comments, please
contact our Customer Care Department within the U.S. at 877-762-
2974, outside the U.S. at 317-572-3993, or fax 317-572-4002.

Some of the people who helped bring this book to market include
the following:

Acquisitions and Editorial

Project Editor: Jodi Jensen

Acquisitions Editor:
Kyle Looper

Copy Editors: Emelie Havard,
Annie Sullivan, Michael Sullivan

Cover image:
©iStockphoto.com/Oleksiy Mark

Composition Services

Sr. Project Coordinator:
Kristie Rees

Layout and Graphics:
Lavonne Roberts,
Christin Swinford

Proofreader:
Dwight Ramsey

Publishing and Editorial for Technology Dummies

Richard Swadley, Vice President and Executive Group Publisher

Andy Cummings, Vice President and Publisher

Mary Bednarek, Executive Acquisitions Director

Mary C. Corder, Editorial Director

Publishing for Consumer Dummies

Kathleen Nebenhaus, Vice President and Executive Publisher

Composition Services

Debbie Stailey, Director of Composition Services

Introduction

● ●

*T*housands upon thousands of iPhone and iPad apps are available in the App Store, with thousands more added each month. No single human (or even a rather large *team* of humans) can look at them all, much less give every one of them a thorough workout. But in this little book, we've tried to give you a taste of some of these apps.

About This Book

We've included the apps we found to be extremely useful, convenient, feature-packed, and just plain fun to use. In trying to narrow down the field, we looked for apps that had achieved some measure of acclaim, a combination of iTunes Store ranking, positive buzz on the web, and iTunes Store reviews. Then, we tossed in the opinions of friends, colleagues, and family members.

Next, we placed each app in a category. Some apps could easily fit into more than one category, but we hope you'll agree with where we've placed them.

In each of the six parts (*categories*) in this book, apps appear alphabetically and are not ranked in any way. Different apps offer different functionality and features, of course; otherwise, think of them all as more or less equally incredible.

Icons Used in This Book

Useful icons appear in the left margins throughout this book. Consider these icons miniature road signs, telling you something extra about the topic at hand. Here's what the three icons used in this book look like and mean.

 These are the juicy morsels, shortcuts, and recommendations that might make the task at hand faster or easier.

 This icon emphasizes the stuff we think you ought to retain. You may even jot down a note to yourself in your iPhone or iPad.

 You wouldn't intentionally run a stop sign, would you? In the same fashion, ignoring warnings may be hazardous to your iPhone or iPad and (by extension) your wallet.

Just One More Thing . . .

We've listed prices for each app, and these prices were accurate at the time this book went to press. That said, developers change App prices regularly, and apps sometimes go on sale. So the price you see in the book may not be the same as the price you see in the App Store.

Part I

Productivity Apps

• •

Do It (Tomorrow) $4.99

*I*t doesn't get much simpler than Do It (Tomorrow) for jotting down things you need to do. Tapping an item marks it as complete. Alternatively, you can tap the right-hand arrow alongside the item to shrug off the task till tomorrow (which I did to the to-do item reminding me to write this chapter for more tomorrows than I care to admit). Flick to the left to see tomorrow's list — which is exactly where any items you don't complete today automatically end up at the stroke of midnight.

 You can get a free version for your computer, but the $4.99 version for your iPhone or iPad lets you stay in sync across your devices and offers the capability to reorder your to-do items any way you want.

Dropbox Free

Dropbox is software that syncs your files online and across your computers. You can use it to synchronize files among as many Mac, Windows, or Linux computers as you want. You can use it to share files with anyone you want. And you can use it to back up important documents.

You create a free Dropbox account and install the free Dropbox software on your computers. A folder named (what else) *Dropbox* appears on each computer; all files you put in the Dropbox folder on Computer 1 are instantly available in the Dropbox folder on Computer 2, and vice versa. Because Dropbox stores those files on its own secure servers, you can access them from anywhere with any web browser.

With the Dropbox *app*, you can use the Internet connection on your device to view the files in your computer's Dropbox folder. You can also specify "favorite" files that are copied automatically to your iPad or iPhone so you can access them without an Internet connection, and you can e-mail links to the files in your Dropbox so your friends can download them.

The Dropbox app lets you view files from these programs: Microsoft Office (Word, Excel, and PowerPoint); Apple iWork (Pages, Numbers, and Keynote); PDFs; most types of image files such as JPEG, TIFF, and PNG; as well as music and video files. You can also upload photos or movies from your iPhone to your Dropbox folder.

Evernote Free ($5/month or $45/year for Premium Ed.)

When it comes to note-taking, Evernote (see Figure 1-1) lets you capture just about any kind of note you can think of, including text, handwritten, photo, e-mail, voice, PDF, and web page notes. Notes you create are automatically synchronized in the cloud, which means they're always up to date no matter where, when, or how you access them: via your iPhone or iPad, the Evernote app on your PC or Mac, or by logging in to the Evernote website at www.evernote.com.

The iPhone and iPad apps with basic service (you get a few thousand notes per month) are free. You can upgrade to the premium plan for more features such as faster uploads and video note capability.

Figure 1-1: Evernote lets you sync notes across gadgets.

GoodReader $4.99

At its heart, GoodReader is a robust PDF reader, capable of handling very large files containing complex images, zooming in and out, and rotating from portrait to landscape (even two-page spreads). GoodReader also lets you open and view documents, presentations, and spreadsheets from Microsoft Office and iWork, HTML or Safari web archives, high-resolution images, audio, and video.

GoodReader's rich feature set is its real appeal, however. You can, for example, annotate a PDF with sticky notes, underlines, highlighting, strikethrough, or even by drawing on the PDF with your finger. You can then share the annotated copy via e-mail, Google Docs, Dropbox, iDisk, or a variety of other methods, while retaining the pristine original. You can follow hyperlinks within a PDF document, search for text within a PDF, or highlight words to look up via dictionary.com, Wikipedia, or Google. You can even crop large PDF page margins with a special crop tool.

GoodReader also aids you in finding documents on the web, connecting to and syncing with a variety of servers, organizing documents and PDFs into folders on the iPhone and iPad, and securing sensitive information via password options for the application and for individual files and folders.

iThoughts $7.99 iPhone/$9.99 iThoughts HD for iPad

When you engage in *mind mapping,* you use a diagram
to show the structure of an idea or plan and highlight
the relationships between different aspects of that idea
or plan. Many mind-mapping apps are available for Mac
and Windows, but only a few (so far) are on the iPad
and iPhone. The dedicated iThoughts mind-mapping
app is the best one I've found, and it has easy-to-use
tools for quickly developing your own maps.

Keynote $9.99

As the second leg of Apple's iWork productivity suite,
Keynote allows you to make presentations directly on
your device. It offers text formatting and image manipu-
lation, professional-looking templates, transitions, and
great controls that make working with this app easy,
fast, and fun. Many of Keynote's conventions mirror
those in Pages, so if you're comfy in one, you'll be
pretty comfy in the other. Even if you're brand-new to
making presentations and leery of this touchscreen
thing, you'll still make a better-looking presentation
with Keynote on your iPhone or iPad than anyone ever
has with PowerPoint on a PC.

Numbers $9.99

Numbers is Apple's spreadsheet app for its iWork suite, but I've never thought of it as a direct competitor to Microsoft Excel. Instead, it's more of a home-and-small-business spreadsheet app with an emphasis on turning data into great-looking graphs and charts. Numbers on iPhone and iPad takes that a little farther by adding some viewing features that make the app good for using completed spreadsheets to get more data. As with Pages and Keynote, Apple has redesigned the interface with the touchscreen in mind, and it's remarkably easy to do things like tie a graph to a spreadsheet and manipulate the fields until you have what you need.

Pages $9.99

Pages is word-processing software from Apple. It can't do *everything* Microsoft Word can do — it's aimed more at consumers than business users — but what it does, it does extremely well. Letters, résumés, thank-you notes and cards, newsletters, proposals, reports, term papers, even posters and flyers. The app is intended to be used with pinches, zooms, swipes, and gestures.

In Pages, Apple made context king. The tools available on the screen depend entirely on what you're doing or have selected, which keeps the app from becoming cluttered. When you're working on your document, the iPad or iPhone screen's real estate is filled with that document, not with tools and palettes you're not using (see Figure 1-2).

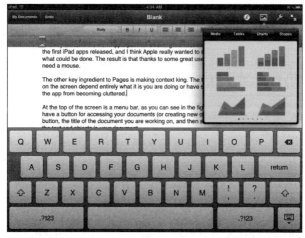

Figure 1-2: The Pages menu bar and helpful buttons.

PowerME HD

$29.99

If you manage projects, consider buying PowerME HD. This handy (though not cheap) app helps you organize your workflow, collaborate with team members, and sync all your plans in the cloud. If you're a mobile professional, these tools come in handy for keeping track of your work and your team's activities. Create and manage projects, juggle deadlines, and organize tasks in your PowerME inbox. Check out the Drawing feature, which can quickly change your old way of creating a preliminary plan by jotting it down on a napkin in a hotel coffee shop. The latest version adds integration with Google Docs and Dropbox, as well as the capability to record and play back movies.

Print Agent $3.99 iPhone/$5.99 iPad

This handy little app lets you view, share, and print documents from your iPhone and iPad. You can send files wirelessly to your printer using the printer's AirPrint capabilities. You can print e-mails, PDF files, and documents from Mail, iWork, or the Microsoft Office suite. And a recent upgrade to this app now lets you connect to Dropbox and print files from there.

If your printer doesn't have AirPrint capability, try checking the web for update's to your printer's drivers. You may find that updates to the printer software will enable this app to work with your printer. How convenient to send files from your iPad or iPhone to your printer from just about anywhere in your house.

Part II

Business and Finance Apps

● ●

Bloomberg   Free (Ad-Supported)

The Bloomberg news organization is not only emerging as one of the most important financial news outlets on the planet (remember, Bloomberg's *core* business is providing financial data to Wall Street and other traders), it's also one of the few major news organizations of any type that has been *adding* reporters to its payroll in the last couple of years.

Here's what you get with this app: Financial news, stock quotes, major indices from around the world, currency information, bond prices, the capability to track your stock portfolio, and access to a lot of market-related podcasts.

 If you've bought shares in a particular company at various times, you can add that stock more than once so you can keep track of the different purchase prices of your holdings.

CamScanner

Free

CamScanner turns your iPhone into a portable scanner. You can scan multi-page documents, including receipts, notes, contracts, invoices, scripts, business cards, and whiteboard discussions. The app's built-in technology ensures that scanned images are perfectly clear and recognizable. Once scanned, you can fax, e-mail, or upload the files to Evernote, GoogleDocs, or iCloud.

CamScanner not only scans documents but also captures notes and images from a whiteboard. And you can add tags to your documents to enable easy searching.

 For $4.99 you can buy CamScanner+, which removes the advertisements you see in the free version and provides PDF files that are watermark-free.

Delivery Status Touch

$4.99

If you do much mail-order buying or shipping, Delivery Status Touch is worth every penny of the nearly $5 price tag. This super-smart app automatically determines the shipper based on a tracking number you copy from confirmation e-mails or shipping page details. Notifications let you know what's what with your package, from processing to shipping status to expected arrival and final delivery.

An optional (and free) Dashboard Widget for Mac lets you track the same info on your notebook or desktop Mac, and any deliveries you enter on either of those or the companion website are automatically added and updated no matter which one you're viewing.

E*TRADE Mobile Pro   Free

With E*TRADE Mobile Pro (see Figure 2-1), you can buy and sell stocks and options, transfer money around on your E*TRADE accounts, set up and manage watch lists, monitor your orders, manage and receive alerts, monitor your portfolio, and get stock quotes and news — all from within this very well-designed and elegant app.

Most of these features require an E*TRADE account. You can't buy or sell stocks, for instance, without such an account, and you can't have a portfolio of stocks or get alerts. Even without an account, however, you can get stock quotes, read company news articles, and monitor the stock indices.

Figure 2-1: Tools and report features in E*TRADE Mobile Pro.

Go To Meeting   Free

If you attend meetings remotely, you'll enjoy this app.
You can use it to join meetings, view presentations,
and take a look at any content a presenter shares with
attendees. Tap a link in an e-mailed invitation, and you
can instantly join a meeting with others using Go To
Meeting via Wi-Fi or 3G/4G. You can also enter the
meeting's phone number, your name, your e-mail, and
then join. After joining you can hear, see, and partici-
pate in meetings.

OmniGraffle $49.99 (iPad only)

OmniGraffle has long been a Mac staple for people who need to make flowcharts, diagrams, and other layout ideas and designs. When the company brought this program to the iPad, they rethought it from the ground up.

This app helps you visually organize your thoughts so that you can present them in a beautiful way. You use tapping, dragging, and multi-touch gestures to draw shapes, create objects, and style your projects until they look just as you had imagined. You can use the built-in stencil collection to quickly create a document, or you can use the various tools to create everything from scratch. OmniGraffle even provides diagramming tools (think organization chart), lets you use lines to connect different shapes, and keeps those connections intact when you move things around!

powerOne Finance Calculator $4.99

The powerOne Finance Calculator app can do complex finance-related calculations for you. And with the included templates, you don't even have to fully understand what you're doing to get the right answer.

This app offers more than 50 templates: some for traders, some for accountants, some for super math people, and some for mere mortals, like me. There's a depreciation template, an inflation calculator, several loan-related calculations, mortgage tools, a sales-tax template, and much more. There's even a tip calculator that will divide your bill among multiple people!

For example, some car dealerships try to sell you a car based on the car payment. That can make it hard to understand how much you're really paying. Or, you may be price-shopping and know the total price, but you want to know what your monthly payment will be. powerOne has a template called Auto Loan that can get you the information you need. As shown in Figure 2-2, to find the monthly payment, you enter the price, sales tax, any fees you might have to pay, the interest rate on your loan, down payment, and the number of months you intend to carry the loan. You get the monthly payment with a simple tap.

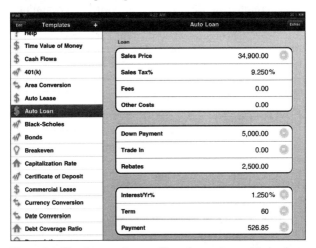

Figure 2-2: Figuring out the specifics of a car loan with the Auto Loan template.

You can work backward, too: Say you want to change what your payment will be. If you enter that, you can tap the equal sign next to any of the other categories and get that figure. For instance, if you want to pay a certain amount per month, you can see how many months you'd need to carry the loan to hit that target. Or if you know how much you can pay per month and how long your bank will carry your note, you can quickly get the figure for how much of a down payment you need to make.

> Don't worry. There is, of course, a standard calculator in this app. Just choose the Calculator template to get a calculator with both math and trig functions. You can tap away on this like you would any ol' calculator.

Prompster Pro $2.99 iPhone/$9.99 iPad

There are several teleprompter apps out there. A couple of them are really good, but I picked Prompster to highlight because it includes an audio recorder built into the app so you can record your presentation as you give it. The basic idea is to use your device display as a portable teleprompter. Import your text from e-mail or through iTunes, or type it up (or edit it) right there on your iPhone or iPad. Set the scrolling speed and the size of your text, and you're off! Onscreen controls let you see the elapsed time, stop as needed, or adjust the speed and text size on the fly.

QuickBooks Mobile Free (iPhone only)

If you're already a paying QuickBooks Online or
QuickBooks for Windows user (sorry, Mac QuickBooks
users!), you can tap into QuickBooks Mobile for free.
Create invoices on the go, add, view, and edit customer
information, and drum up job and sales estimates.
Thanks to the same level of encryption security used
by banks, you can rest assured that your money mat-
ters are protected from unauthorized access when
you're taking care of the business at hand.

Quickoffice Pro $14.99 iPhone/$19.99 iPad

This app is intended for people who are more comfort-
able using Microsoft Word and Excel than Apple's
iWork approach. Quickoffice Pro is built on the same
paradigms as Word and Excel — in fact, its *raison d'être*
is to view, create, and edit files in Microsoft Office file
formats. You can switch among your Mac, PC, iPad,
and iPhone with Word and Excel files, as long as you
use DOC, DOCX, TXT, XLS, XLSX, XLT, and XLTX file
formats. Unless and until Microsoft brings the real deal
to iOS, Quickoffice is the best way to work on your
Office files on the iPad in an Office-y kind of way.

Another useful aspect of Quickoffice is that it has
Dropbox support built into it. The excellent Dropbox
utility gives you access to files on a variety of devices,
including iPad. (I talk about Dropbox in more detail in
Part I.) With Dropbox support in Quickoffice, you can
create a Word document on your PC at work and put it

in your Dropbox. Then, when you're at the coffee shop that afternoon and you need to edit it, simply open it from your Dropbox in Quickoffice on your iPad or iPhone. When you get home to your Mac, you can open the file from Dropbox there, too! Quickoffice also supports Google Docs and Box.

Quick Sale $0.99 iPhone/$9.99 iPad

Quick Sale is a handy app for anyone who needs to invoice on the go (at street fairs, at a client's location, on a business trip, at a trade show, and so on). For that matter, this app is for anyone who wants to interface with customers with an iPhone or iPad in hand instead of a computer. Quick Sale is a fairly complete invoicing solution for your device. It offers unlimited inventory items and services (including photos for each one, if you want, and barcode scanner support) that you can organize by category. It also offers reports and the ability to e-mail reports and invoices.

The iPad version of Quick Sale is a more feature-rich app and gives you the ability to add photos for items. In addition, all invoice labels can be customized for your needs or language, customer information can be accessed from the iPad's contacts list, sales reports can be exported in the CSV file format, and you get seamless integration with the Credit Card Terminal app from Inner Fence.

 You can print invoices directly from your iPad to an AirPrint-compatible wireless printer.

XpenseTracker $4.99

As the name suggests, XpenseTracker lets you track your expenses, both business and personal. It has some nice features, such as remembering your last payment transaction for each category and support for all major currencies.

With XpenseTracker, you can customize the categories and subcategories that work best for you, access a "frequently used" list of the descriptions you use on a regular basis, track your mileage, download daily exchange rates from the web, e-mail your expense reports, and much, much more.

XpenseTracker isn't the only expense-tracking app in the App Store, but it is one of the few that supports Dropbox. Dropbox support costs an extra $0.99 (as an in-app purchase), but if you enjoy the convenience of Dropbox, that is probably $0.99 well spent. Dropbox makes it easy to import and export files from your computer, which can be the key for using this app effectively.

Part III

Travel, Food, and Navigation Apps

• •

FlightTrack Pro — Live Flight Status Tracker by Mobiata
$9.99

*F*lightTrack Pro is great for when you're traveling, but it's also a good app to have when you're expecting friends, family, or business associates who are traveling to you! You can track flights all over the world on a map — more than 16,000 airports and 1400 airlines worldwide are covered. FlightTrack Pro provides real-time status for delays, gates, and cancellations, and you can also view weather forecasts and weather radar.

FlightTrack Pro works seamlessly with TripIt, the third-party service that monitors your flights for you (see the TripIt listing later in this part). You can automatically sync your itinerary with TripIt, as well as syncing with the calendar on your phone.

You can share flight information via e-mail, Facebook, or Twitter directly from the app. You'll appreciate this when you get a Push update about a delayed flight and need to send it to your coworker or family member who is meeting the flight.

Inrix Traffic/Inrix Traffic Pro Free

Inrix Traffic is a free app that provides real-time traffic information and traffic forecasts. It's easy to use, and I use it to avoid traffic whenever I drive more than a few miles from home.

The real-time traffic-flow information it delivers covers major roadways in 126 cities across the U.S. and Canada. The flow of traffic appears on a familiar Google Map you can pinch or unpinch to zoom in to or out of. Traffic moving at or near the speed limit is displayed in green, as are most of the major highways. Moderate traffic is displayed in orange; heavy traffic is shown in red. Traffic incidents — such as construction, road closures, concerts, conventions, sporting events, and so on — are depicted by icons such as a yellow traffic cone. When you tap an icon, you see an overlay with details about the incident.

Another useful feature is traffic prediction. The app analyzes current traffic conditions, time of day, day of the week, holidays, accidents, construction, conventions, sporting events, and more, using the data to predict traffic situations over the next few hours.

Everything I've mentioned is available for free and with no advertising. That's good. And although the app delivers a lot of value for free, you may want to upgrade to the Pro version for $9.99 a year or $24.99 for life, which adds these useful features: the fastest route from Point A to Point B; the expected travel time and your estimated time of arrival (ETA); turn-by-turn directions; the best time to leave Point A so that you have the shortest drive time to Point B; the capability to save your frequent destinations and favorite routes; and access to images from some traffic cameras.

iTranslate   Free/$1.99 without ads

If you travel internationally and don't happen to have mastered seven languages like James Bond, iTranslate might just be a great app to have on your iPad or iPhone. It has an easy-to-use interface: just type a word in the top pane set to a language such as English, and then tap the setting for the second language and scroll to find the one you need, such as Italian. Want to hear the pronunciation? Just tap the little speaker icon in the second language, and the word is pronounced correctly. If you purchase an add-on voice recognition package, you can speak words to the translator. Tap an icon to mark a word or phrase, such as "I'll have a glass of wine," as a favorite, and you can look it up easily anytime you need it. You can even slow down a pronunciation and choose to hear either a male or female voice.

Kayak   Free

Use your iPhone or iPad to tap into all the great things you'll find on the Kayak.com website. Compare rates for flights, hotels, and rental cars; look up baggage fees;

check your flight status; track your flight status; view and manage your trip itinerary; and keep the numbers for airlines and airport information right at your fingertips.

MotionX GPS Drive
$0.99 iPhone/$0.99 iPad (HD)

MotionX GPS Drive is a great value when compared to most voice-guided navigation apps for the iPhone and iPad. For the initial cost of the app, you get 30 days of real-time, turn-by-turn navigation with Live Voice Guidance. When your 30 days are up, you can make an in-app purchase and buy additional Voice Guidance packages by the month or the year.

MotionX GPS Drive (see Figure 3-1) offers these things that I find particularly compelling:

- ✔ The MotionX-3D Plus maps always show the name of the street you're currently on at the bottom of the screen.

- ✔ If I don't need Live Voice Guidance for a month, I don't have to pay for it. I buy it when I need it, with no recurring fees or subscription.

- ✔ The app itself is under 10 MB, and it lets you decide how much storage space you want to use for maps; other navigation apps weigh in at 1.5 GB or more!

- ✔ It features "Smart Router" technology that uses multiple traffic-data sources to calculate the best route in real time.

✔ It's the only GPS navigation package I've tested that offers two simulation modes — step-by-step or automatic — at playback speeds up to 8X. So you can see the entire route, turn by turn, before you even get into your car.

The Search interface is nicely designed, offering categories such as coffee shops, gas stations, dining, and a browse mode that shows you nearby entertainment, restaurant, shopping, and WiFi hotspot options. You can search during an active navigation session and see results that are on your chosen route.

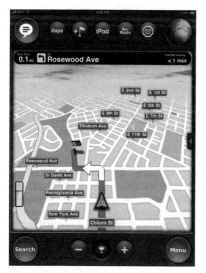

Figure 3-1: Easy-to-read maps and on-screen instructions.

TripIt
Free

If you travel at all, definitely get TripIt. This app takes all your trip information and creates one detailed itinerary that is stored conveniently at your fingertips on your iPhone or iPad. You can sync your information with the calendar on your device, and you can easily set up trips and share itineraries with anyone in your life who needs this information.

TripIt pushes notifications to you of flight delays or gate changes. You can keep track of hotel and even restaurant reservations in one convenient place. In addition, if a better price comes along before you set off on your trip, you might be able to get a refund — all courtesy of TripIt's notifications about the best available fares. TripIt also offers features that help you track your frequent traveler points and get perks such as rental car VIP memberships.

Urbanspoon
Free

How many times have you spent 45 minutes playing the "I don't know, where do *you* want to go?" game with your spouse, your friends, or your workmates? I hate that game, and I can't even begin to tell you how much, but Urbanspoon can change that.

The basic premise of the app is to let you find a restaurant by randomly choosing from various cuisines, price points, and different neighborhoods on three slot machine reels. Shake your iPhone or iPad (or push the "Shake" button) and you get a random suggestion for where to eat. If you don't like the result, shake it again. If you want to limit your options, say to a particular neighborhood or type of food, you can lock one, two, or even all three reels to try to find a particular kind of restaurant.

 Check out the "Show Popular" button at the top left of the map to limit your choices to only restaurants that have been highly rated by Urbanspoon users.

When you get a restaurant you like, just tap its name and you'll see a screen with its address, phone number, kind of restaurant, Urbanspoon user rating, cost rating (indicated by one, two, or three dollar signs), and reviews of the place (where applicable).

Wikihood Plus $4.99 iPhone/$6.99 iPad

Wikihood Plus is an app that taps into that vast reservoir of (mostly accurate) information known as Wikipedia. Using either your current location or a location you choose, Wikihood Plus tells you what's nearby, based on the millions of entries in Wikipedia. The app digs into Wikipedia for you and uses algorithms to sift through that data to show you what's near you, what's significant, and how to get there. Building further on the wiki theme, there are thousands of in-app user ratings.

Here's an example of how you can use this app. Say you're visiting Central Park in New York City and want to check out some attractions in the area. If you open Wikihood Plus and let it use your current location (you'll need an Internet connection), it shows you that the Museum of Natural History's subway stop is right next to you (and the museum itself is close, too). The Hayden Planetarium is also nearby.

 Wikipedia is an encyclopedia comprised of information supplied by its users, and there are hundreds of thousands of contributors around the world! It's accurate more often than not, but if you have any questions, you should probably check with another source to confirm.

Yelp
Free

Yelp lets you find the top-rated taco shop in your neighborhood or read reviews of professional services such as veterinarians and dry cleaning shops. Or, you can quickly uncover the nearest cafe that is open when you need to get your eye-opening java juju on.

Yelp lets you narrow your searches by neighborhood, distance from your current location, price, and what's open now. You can add tips, photos, and reviews for your favorite businesses, read reviews, look up addresses and phone numbers for thousands of businesses, and even make a reservation via OpenTable without leaving Yelp. You can choose to post your check-ins to Facebook and Twitter automatically.

ZAGAT

$9.99

ZAGAT is one of the most comprehensive restaurant guides on the planet, and this app gives you access to thousands of restaurant reviews, a GPS-enabled restaurant locator, the capability to search for restaurants according to multiple criteria, and more. This is definitely a must-have app for foodies and is constantly updated with new reviews.

ZAGAT is not a crowd-sourced guide, so its reviews are limited to major metropolitan areas. That means you should check to make sure the areas where you're intending to use the app are actually covered.

ZAGAT lets you pick a city or use your device's Location Services to determine your current location. The interface itself is almost entirely dominated by a Google Maps display of the area, with ZAGAT-reviewed restaurants highlighted with Z pins. Tap a pin, and you get a pane at the top of the screen with basic information about the place, including its name, food, décor, service ratings on a scale of 0–30, and the average cost of a meal (including one drink and a tip). You'll also find the beginning of the ZAGAT review, which will often be enough to let you know whether you want to eat there.

In Figure 3-2, I'm looking at restaurants in Brooklyn, where I found The Grocery. It has a stunning 27 rating for its food, although it's rather pricey at $60 per meal.

Figure 3-2: The Grocery is a highly rated restaurant in Brooklyn.

Part IV

Social Networking and Communication Apps

• •

Facebook   Free

*T*he Facebook app gives you all the usual tools for keeping in touch with friends. Update your status, post a photo, and read and comment on others' postings no matter where you are. Peruse your notifications, messages, and friend requests, play your favorite Facebook games on the go, and stay connected to your Facebook apps. Use the Nearby app to see what your friends are up to. Stay in touch and continue building your network!

Flipboard   Free

Flipboard provides a visual way to organize and view all the information that's coming at you through a variety of sites and sources.

Flipboard is quite simply a nicely designed, graphical, magazine-style interface for accessing blogs, postings, and news in one place. Each item you're following displays in a section on the Flipboard home page (as shown in Figure 4-1).

Figure 4-1: Recent Twitter posts laid out magazine style.

Sign in to your Facebook or Twitter account and add a Flipboard section on a person to follow in the news, as well as view their online postings. You can add sections from the home page by tapping a blank block sporting the words *Add a Section*. You can also tap the Featured tab, tap some featured content to open that page, and then tap the Add to Contents button to add it as a section in Flipboard Contents.

In adding sections for Flipboard (you're limited to nine items on a page, but you can use your finger to flip to the next page to add more sections), you can choose a persona, list, or blog from Twitter for easy access to that content.

 To delete a section that doesn't interest you, tap the Edit button and use the Delete buttons that appear on each section to delete one or more.

FourSquare   Free (for iPhone)

Explore your surroundings, check-in at venues, read tips and reviews of those places you check in to — and even unlock discounts and rewards. Each check-in boosts your cred among friends and locals. Feel free to snap pictures to enhance venue information. Integration with Facebook and Twitter means you can automatically post your check-ins to those services if you choose.

1M+   Free

This instant messaging app works with Google Talk, Yahoo! Messenger, MSN/Windows Live Messenger, AIM/iChat, ICQ, Myspace, Twitter, Facebook, and Jabber. You can share text, photos, voice, and video, and organize your various IM messages easily. There are several really attractive backgrounds to choose from to customize your IM environment, making chats an appealing visual experience. You can also see at a glance which of your contacts is online at any moment.

IM+ is free, but you do get ads. If you want the advertisement-free version, fork over $9.99 for IM+ Pro. That version adds a handy conversation history feature and Skype chat.

LinkedIn
Free

Social networking becomes professional networking with the LinkedIn app. This app lets you share information with your network, connect with more than 161 million users worldwide, recommend colleagues or request recommendations from them, and stay up-to-date on industry news.

 If you have a special interest, chances are there's a LinkedIn group for you. Just search for your special interest to find others who share that interest.

Skype
Free

Besides giving you the capability of free or low-fee voice calling, the Skype app lets you conduct face-to-face video chats with other "Skypers" running the mobile app or running Skype on their Mac or Windows PC (see Figure 4-2). To see each other at the same time, your smartphone must be equipped with a front-facing camera like the one found on iPhone 4 and later models.

You can make Skype calls to your Skype contacts for free via Wi-Fi or 3G. You can also keep in touch with instant messaging via Skype. This can cut down or even eliminate costly text messaging plans if the people you text with the most are running the Skype app on their smartphones.

Figure 4-2: Be seen *and* heard with Skype.

Twitter Free

I love the Twitter app, and I think it offers the single best Twitter experience on either device. From usability to readability, general layout, and design, it's a great app.

Look at the left part of Figure 4-3. In portrait mode, you get two panels. The left panel has a list of your Twitter accounts with tabs for your Timeline (tweets from you and those you follow), @Mentions (tweets with your @ Name in them), Lists, Messages, and a tab for viewing and editing your own Profile, and one for Search. To the right is a pane for your tweets. At the bottom of the page is a Settings button and a New Tweet button.

All those elements are logically laid out; but what sets this app apart is the way those elements can be expanded, pushed, pinched, and swiped — making the best use of your screen real estate at any given time.

You can reply, repost, quote, translate (seriously, one-tap translation!), or just copy a link that shows up in a tweet.

Lastly, there's a built-in browser for displaying photos and links. At the bottom of the browser is a button that lets you open the link in Safari.

Twitterific for Twitter Free

If you live to tweet, you should check out Twitterific for Twitter. Each tweet offers access to a set of tools you can use to reply to the tweet, retweet, or retweet with comment. There are tools that let you translate a tweet or e-mail it. You can also display tweets in conversations to help you follow along with the crowd.

Figure 4-3: Twitter's layout on your device.

Don't have time to read all your favorite tweets in real time? If you want to keep track of tweets even when you're offline, you'll like the easy interaction Twitterific has with Instapaper, a $4.99 app you can use to save pages of content to read later, at your leisure.

Use the Trends feature (like the Top Trending Topics you see on Twitter's own site) to view some of the hottest Twitter topics, such as conversations about the latest developments on your favorite TV show or sports team.

Part V

Cooking, Health, and Fitness Apps

- -

All-in YOGA

$0.99

All-in YOGA has a database of 200 poses with images and instructions on how to perform the poses, two built-in programs that will custom-build a routine to match your abilities, goals, and time commitment, the option to build your own routines, a journaling feature that tracks your workouts, and a very good in-app Help system.

Each skill level has two rows of poses that you can scroll through with a swipe. When you tap on a pose, you get directions for the pose, a photo of how the pose should look, and an audio button. Most of them also have a tappable video showing the pose in action.

 The main poses have a 3D muscle view that shows you which muscles are stretched when doing the pose.

When you start a workout, you see a large image of the pose with a countdown timer for how long you should spend doing it (see Figure 5-1). A voice offers specific instructions and music begins playing. When it's time to move to the next pose, the image changes and the timer resets. There are onscreen controls that let you pause the program, get instructions for the current pose, turn off the voice or music, and watch a video (for poses that include a video).

Figure 5-1: The countdown timer is a great feature.

Calorie Counter and Diet Tracker
Free

With over 1.1 million types of food in the Calorie Counter database, counting calories has never been so easy. This app also has built-in food and exercise calculators that accurately predict how many calories you are burning. In addition, the application comes with a free barcode scanner to use to determine calorie and nutrition content. You can even insert your own recipe and the app will calculate the calories! For anyone on a strict diet or trying to lose a little weight, this app is extremely helpful by calculating how many calories you are taking in and how many you are losing.

The exercise portion of the app offers 350 exercises as well as evaluates and reports your cardio and strength training and conditioning.

Epicurious Recipes & Shopping List
Free (Ad Supported)

Epicurious is a recipe app "for people who love to eat." The app offers several ways to browse for recipes. For instance, there are ten different categories, from Summer Dinners to Decadent Desserts. When you pick a category, the screen offers an easy-to-read list of the recipes in that category, with tabs on the far right that provide sorting options for the list.

At the bottom of each Recipe screen are tabs for Reviews and About (info about the author); if the recipe offers nutritional information, you'll see a third tab for that.

There's a Search button so you can search for recipes in several ways: by Main Ingredient, Meal/Course, Cuisines, Dietary Consideration, Dish Type, and Season or Occasion.

We're still not done, though, because there's also a shopping-list feature. Just tap a button and you get a shopping list with the precise amounts of everything you need to prepare that dish.

How to Cook Everything $9.99

The How to Cook Everything app has over 2,000 recipes that come complete with over 400 illustrations, preparation steps, technique advice, and creative ideas. To make cooking even easier, this app utilizes built-in timers that operate even after closing the program. Easy search menus make it convenient to search for new and easy recipes.

Users can also easily print recipes and e-mail up to 10 recipes a month to friends, family, and coworkers. The app also has a very handy shopping list for ingredients and allows you to plan meals on a calendar.

iFitness $0.99 iPhone/$1.99 iPad

Here's an app I've always needed. iFitness offers more than 300 exercises; you can use it to track your workouts, your weight and/or size (whether you're trying to get bigger or smaller); and it includes a built-in Body Mass Index (BMI) Calculator.

This app's standout feature, however, is its photographs and instructions on how to do the exercises and how to use the machines in your gym (see Figure 5-2).

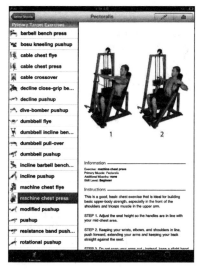

Figure 5-2: Get instructions for using a machine properly.

 iFitness supports multiple profiles so more than one person can track workouts.

In the Exercises tab, exercises are grouped according to abdominals, arms, back, chest, legs, and shoulders, as well as cardio exercises and stretches. You can also see exercises grouped according to the equipment used.

Once you know your exercises, you can choose from built-in routines. There are also routines built for specific sports (such as golf or hockey) and for targeting specific parts of the body. You can also build your own routine and assemble exercises you want to do.

You can record weight and reps for each exercise — the results of which are logged and graphed if you're also entering your weight and other profile information. Or, you can use the app without entering this information.

Navy SEAL Fitness $1.99

Come on, you mean I can work out like a Navy SEAL? Okay, *I* couldn't get through a Navy SEAL workout, but maybe you can. This app is based on The Navy SEAL Physical Fitness Guide developed by the U.S. Navy for its elite special forces. Accordingly, it has a lot of information about fitness, exercises, how and why those exercises work, conditioning, and how to work out to achieve the high level of fitness expected of Navy SEALs.

Nike+ Running Free

The Nike+ Running app helps you plan runs or bike rides, set time intervals, track progress and distance, and record past times to show improvement. With amazing map displays, planning runs, bike rides, and marathon training has never been so easy. The app also has little motivational boosts like cheers that play when your friends comment and like your status, and it offers voice feedback during your run to tell you how you're doing. Aside from receiving motivational boosts, you can also activate your personal "PowerSongs" to motivate you to push harder and break your own records. Nike+ Running can even calculate the calories you burn during your workout. This app is convenient and useful for anyone who enjoys exercising and running outside.

Prognosis: Your Diagnosis   Free

The Prognosis: Your Diagnosis app is an enthralling cartoon-based game that allows the user to diagnose clinical cases. This app has over 750,000 users worldwide, and it's excellent for students interested in the medical field, medical professionals, and as practice for the Medical College Admission Test (MCAT). Each game's information is based on real patients and each case is checked by a panel of medical experts. While providing entertainment, this app can teach beginners the basics of medicine and help doctors and nurses hone their skills. With a new case added every week, you can play doctor and diagnose, evaluate, and make decisions about treating patients. After each completed case, the app gives an explanation of what the doctor should have done to help improve diagnosis and treatment skills.

Prognosis: Your Diagnosis is an amusing and enjoyable app that can help both medical novices and true professionals hone their diagnosis skills in a fun way.

Weber's on the Grill $4.99

This app has a lot of recipes for grilling and BBQ-ing, and those recipes have gorgeous pictures and easy-to-follow directions. But there's more, most especially a series of How-Tos that covers everything from grilling basics to individual cooking techniques. Even better still is that some of the How-To's are videos created by celebrity chef and cookbook author Jamie Purviance.

Let's start with the Recipes, the *raison d'être* of this app. You can browse by category, such as Starters, Red Meat, Seafood, Rubs, Marinades, and such, or search for ingredients or other keywords.

Tap a recipe, and it appears on the screen. You're told how many the recipe serves, how much prep time you'll need, how much time for marinating or other post-prep, grilling time, and a list of any special equipment (like bamboo skewers) you might need. There's also a detailed ingredient list, a photo of the finished dish, and step-by-step instructions for making the dish, which you can see in Figure 5-3.

At the top of each recipe is an icon for adding it to your Favorites, generating a shopping list, or e-mailing it to someone else.

Figure 5-3: Step-by-step instructions and a list of ingredients make cooking easy with this app.

WebMD Free

WebMD allows you to look up symptoms and conditions, research drugs, and browse first-aid information. The app also provides a Google Maps-based component for finding healthcare services, including physicians, hospitals, and pharmacies.

On the Home page, you'll find buttons for Symptom Checker, Conditions, Drugs & Treatments, First Aid Information, Local Health Listings, and an About tab.

Tap on the Symptoms Checker, and you'll get a picture of a naked Ken or Barbie Doll, along with a request to enter your profile (Age, Sex, Zip Code). Touch this avatar where you're experiencing symptoms, and you'll get a popup window with symptoms pertinent to that specific part of the body. Choose a symptom, answer some questions, and you'll be given some extensive information about what might be causing the symptom, as well as some links to related articles.

One of the most important features in this app is the extensive database of prescription drugs. Each drug has information about how it's used, what it's pre-scribed for, the side effects, precautions you should take, interaction issues, and what to do in case of an overdose.

Lastly, the Google Maps-powered Listings page comes in handy when you need to find a doctor, hospital, or pharmacy near you.

Part VI

News, Weather, and Entertainment Apps

● ●

Angry Birds   Free

*T*he object of Angry Birds is to shoot birds from a slingshot-like apparatus (see Figure 6-1) to knock down structures and kill the green pigs who have stolen the birds' eggs. Kill all green pigs on a level and you get to advance; but leave even one little green piggy alive, and you'll have to redo the level. On each level, you get a fixed number of birds. The birds are your weapons. Aim your bird carefully and be sure you don't pull the slingshot back too much or too little. Different birds have different attributes. Little blue birds, for example, divide into three individual blue birds when you tap while they're in flight. The yellow triangular birds double their speed when you tap while they're flying. The big white egg-shaped birds drop an egg-shaped bomb when you tap.

 Your primary objective may be to destroy the pigs using the fewest missiles (birds), but you'll usually have to destroy structures and other stuff to get to the pigs.

Figure 6-1: Use the slingshot to send birds careening through the air.

Instapaper $3.99

Instapaper is a capable RSS newsreader that allows you to tag articles, websites, Flickr pics, and just about everything else on the web for viewing later when you have a moment to spare.

This app allows you to browse RSS feeds, each with its own folder. When browsing your feeds, you can either read the articles right then and there or save them to your Read Later folder. Each article in Instapaper has a link to the original posting on the web, allowing you to view the article with its original formatting and layout, including any ads that paid for it.

 If you're in another app that supports Instapaper, you can add items to your Read Later folder from within that app. This is handy for offline viewing, but it's especially great if you're going through a lot of tweets and want to gather everything together to read later.

Movies by Flixster Free

Movies by Flixster lets you look up an intriguing movie and get critic and viewer reviews, as well as photos and information about the cast and director. But what I really like about this app is that you can tap the Showtimes button and find out where this picture is playing near you, and when. You can then get a map to theaters to find your way there. You can comment on a movie on Facebook or play a trailer. Tap a link to go to Rotten Tomatoes, the review site run by Flixster. You can also look up the latest movies by what's most popular, by title, or by rating.

Netflix Free (subscription required)

You may already know that Netflix started life as a mail-based DVD rental service. For a monthly subscription, you can have DVDs of TV shows and movies delivered to your house. After you watch and return them, Netflix sends you the next DVD in your queue. The quicker you return the disc, the faster you get the next one, so the more bang for your buck.

Then, Netflix started adding services, such as streaming movies and TV shows. With this handy app, and for
your monthly Netflix fee, you can choose from thousands of TV shows and movies to watch on your
iPhone or iPad — any time you want, as often as you
want — as long as you have an Internet connection.
You can even begin watching on one device and then
switch to a different device.

NPR News/NPR for iPad Free

The NPR (National Public Radio) app offers you access
to just about everything NPR produces, including writ-
ten stories, radio news stories, and a broad selection of
entertainment and informational radio shows.

You can browse NPR's content in several ways. The
home screen features three scrollable timelines, one
each for News, Arts & Life, and Music. These three
streams are all stories and articles produced by the
NPR news organization — the different radio programs
are offered separately. You can swipe through these
three streams from left to right. When you tap a story
that interests you, it takes over the screen, with the
category stream at the bottom.

Some of these articles are offered in text only, but most
of them have an accompanying radio report embedded
right there. You can listen to the audio report from the
home screen by tapping the speaker button in the
teaser or by tapping the Listen Now button in the full
article. You can also queue up stories in a Playlist for
later listening.

The NPR app also offers up about 20 of its radio programs. If you tap the Programs button at the bottom of the screen, you get a pop-up window with each program listed. Tap a show, and you get a list of the current and recent episodes you can play or add to a playlist. If it has a podcast version on iTunes, you'll find a button for getting it there, too!

Pandora Radio   Free

Pandora Radio is the self-titled app that brings the Pandora streaming radio service from your browser to your iPad and iPhone.

Here's how it works, in the online service as well as the iPhone and iPad app: When you first launch Pandora, you're prompted to sign in with an existing account or create a new one. After you sign in, you can create a new station by simply searching for a band (or song or artist). When you do, Pandora starts playing a song by that band. You can give that song a thumbs-up or a thumbs-down. Pandora then looks at the songs you like (and don't like) and plays other songs it thinks you will like based on what people with similar tastes have said they like. This allows you to train your stations to play music you're probably going to really enjoy, but you're still going to hear music you've never heard before!

You can create as many stations as you want (and even shuffle among them). If a station gets out of control for you, delete it and start a new one. In Figure 6-2, I have set up stations for The Brian Jonestown Massacre, The Who, The Beatles, Led Zeppelin, Black Rebel Motorcycle Club, The Church, and a band called Jucifer.

Figure 6-2: List on left shows radio stations set up; right side shows information about the song currently playing.

See that I gave this song a thumbs-up, from the icon next to the name of the band. If I tap the Menu button directly below it, I can bookmark the song or artist, and I can also get taken straight to the song or artist in iTunes!

Pandora is free, but it limits you to 40 hours of listening per month, a limit relating to a royalty agreement between the station and rights holders. For most users, 40 hours per month will probably be enough. For $36 per year, you can have unlimited listening time, no ads, and a desktop app for listening to Pandora without a browser on your computer.

Pulse News

Free

Pulse allows you to create your own RSS feed made up of articles you choose. Pulse's main view offers four rows of squares — each row representing a different RSS feed, and each square representing a different article in that feed, including any images. You swipe horizontally to browse through all your feeds, and you swipe vertically to browse through an individual feed.

When you tap any particular article, all the other feeds disappear, and the full RSS listing takes over the rest of the page. To read more, tap the headline or the Web button at the top right of the screen. That activates the built-in browser, which pulls up the web-based version of the full article.

This app looks best in landscape mode. In fact, the developers designed it for "two thumbs" mode because that's how they saw people using it on their iPads in coffee shops!

To manage your RSS feeds, you can enter any RSS feed URL directly, or you can do a search. Pulse then taps into Google and returns only the results with RSS feeds that pertain to your search. Then tap the one you want and it's added to Pulse!

SkyGrid

Free

SkyGrid is a phenomenal application that helps you personalize the news stories you receive. This app saves time by aggregating many different news sources onto one personalized screen so that you don't have to

check dozens of websites to find the news that interests you. SkyGrid lets you customize information about
your interests and the topics you like, and the information is updated and displayed when your main page is
loaded. SkyGrid makes finding news effortless, and it
even has instant post options to Facebook and Twitter
to show all your friends the latest news stories.

The What's Hot option tracks the highest-
trending stories so you don't miss any important breaking news.

The Weather Channel Free

The Weather Channel app has forecasts, weather maps,
warnings, and even some weather videos. The app also
has ads, which turns off some people. But you're getting a
lot of content for free, and those ads pay for that content.

When you first launch the app, it asks whether it can
use your current location (assuming you have your
device set to ask for that permission). If you tap OK,
you see the home screen showing the temperature for
the city you've set as your home location. You should
also see buttons for different features of the app: Map,
Video, Weather, Social, In Season.

The Map button shows your current location on a
Google map. If you press the Layers button (it looks
like three stacked squares), you can choose to add an
overlay to the map for Radar, Clouds, Radar & Clouds,
Temperature, Feels Like, 24 Hr Rainfall, 24 Hr Snowfall,
and UV Index.

The Video button offers some must-see weather videos.
The Weather button presents a strip that gives you

options to see weather Now, Hourly, 36 Hour, or 10 Day. The Social button gives you access to The Weather Channel-related Twitter feeds, and the In Season button shows you such things as the forecasted pollen level for your area.

 If you want to change your home location or add other locations, press the *i* button and make your changes on the Settings screen.

TuneIn Radio
Free

TuneIn Radio lets you listen to more than 60,000 AM and FM radio stations from around the world, as well as stations close to home. A handy radio guide helps you find shows and stations you're interested in, and pause and rewind features mean you'll never miss a beat . . . or word.

With this app, you can tune in to streams from ESPN, BBC, CBS, TEDTalks, and more. You can search by song, artist, or show and find a station playing it live somewhere in the world. You can also set up your favorite stations as presets, and the alarm and sleep timer features let you wake up or fall asleep to your favorite music or shows.

Words With Friends
Free

Words With Friends is a lot like Scrabble, but you play against your friends or random strangers asynchronously. You make a word; then it's your opponent's turn. After your opponent makes a word, it's your turn again. Repeat until no tiles remain in your rack(s).

It has all your favorite Scrabble features — including double and triple word and letter scores. The tiles have the same point values as in Scrabble, so you already know how to play! You can play up to 20 games simultaneously.